THE PUPPET MASTER
By Dwayne Jeffery

Copyright © 2009 by Dwayne Jeffery, All rights reserved.
ISBN: 1-60003-444-6

CAUTION: Professionals and amateurs are hereby warned that this Work is subject to a royalty. This Work is fully protected under the copyright laws of the United States of America and all countries with which the United States has reciprocal copyright relations, whether through bilateral or multilateral treaties or otherwise, and including, but not limited to, all countries covered by the Pan-American Copyright Convention, the Universal Copyright Convention and the Berne Convention.

RIGHTS RESERVED: All rights to this Work are strictly reserved, including professional and amateur stage performance rights. Also reserved are: motion picture, recitation, lecturing, public reading, radio broadcasting, television, video or sound recording, all forms of mechanical or electronic reproduction, such as CD-ROM, CD-I, DVD, information and storage retrieval systems and photocopying, and the rights of translation into non-English languages.

PERFORMANCE RIGHTS AND ROYALTY PAYMENTS: All amateur and stock performance rights to this Work are controlled exclusively by Brooklyn Publishers, LLC. No amateur or stock production groups or individuals may perform this play without securing license and royalty arrangements in advance from Brooklyn Publishers, LLC. Questions concerning other rights should be addressed to Brooklyn Publishers, LLC. Royalty fees are subject to change without notice. Professional and stock fees will be set upon application in accordance with your producing circumstances. Any licensing requests and inquiries relating to amateur and stock (professional) performance rights should be addressed to Brooklyn Publishers, LLC.

Royalty of the required amount must be paid, whether the play is presented for charity or profit and whether or not admission is charged.

AUTHOR CREDIT: All groups or individuals receiving permission to produce this play must give the author(s) credit in any and all advertisement and publicity relating to the production of this play. The author's billing must appear directly below the title on a separate line where no other written matter appears. The name of the author(s) must be at least 50% as large as the title of the play. No person or entity may receive larger or more prominent credit than that which is given to the author(s).

PUBLISHER CREDIT: Whenever this play is produced, all programs, advertisements, flyers or other printed material must include the following notice:

Produced by special arrangement with Brooklyn Publishers, LLC

COPYING: Any unauthorized copying of this Work or excerpts from this Work is strictly forbidden by law. No part of this Work may be reproduced, stored in a retrieval system, or transmitted in any form, by any means now known or yet to be invented, including photocopying or scanning, without prior permission from Brooklyn Publishers, LLC.

CHARACTERS
(7 female. 5 male)

MARKUS	A bit of a stoner
HELENA	A poet
KAREN	Superficial Cheerleader
ROBYN	The school gossip
TAMARA	Shy insecure girl
ETHAN	Semi-popular guy
SARAH	Average teen girl
JEREMY	A rock and roller
MIRANDA	Academic girl
CHANCE	Quarterback
TISH	Lost girl
ADAM	Angry boy

TIME: Present day

SETTING: A bare stage with 12 stools

MUSIC / SOUND: The play can be done with no music or sound effects or using director's choices can add music.

LIGHTING: The lighting will be critical, as spotlights will focus on the character (s) speaking.

THE PUPPET MASTER
by
Dwayne Jeffery

SCENE ONE

Curtain opens.

MARKUS: *(Dials his cell and speaks)* Hey dude. *(Pause)* No, you just called me. *(Pause)* Dude, no, you just called me. *(Pause)* Dude, no, you just called ... *(Pause- looks at phone)* Oh. *(Laughs)* Why did I call you? *(Pause)* Well if you don't know how am I supposed to know? *(Pause)* OK, yeah later, I kinda got the munchies anyway. *(Closes cell phone)*

HELENA: It was the best of times
It was the worst of times
It was the wasted generation
It was a youth led segregation
Lives are labelled early on
A puzzle piece, a willing pawn
The puppet master stirred the pot
While social conscience began to rot
So watch along as we re-create
Your generation's self-inflicted fate.

MARKUS: It was like ... you know ... not good.

KAREN: It is not easy being a popular trend setter. Everyone watches your every move; everyone wants to be you. You need the right hair, right clothes, right look and the right body. *(Poses)* Plus the pressure to always be on and in the know is a lot of work. That said, high school is a sweet time. I love watching the eye candy, flirting with the football players, going to cheerleading practice and hanging out with my posse. Of course, like all teenagers, I love to hear the latest rumour and enjoy adding my two cents worth. What is the harm?

ROBYN: OK, let's get one thing straight. Did you see Cruel Intentions? If you did, I compare myself to the Sarah Michelle Gellar character. I like to manipulate; to connive; I get pleasure out of other's pain; I revel in the universal suffering of others.

MARKUS: *(Covering his words with a cough)* Psycho.

TAMARA: So I was always perceived as the shy one, because I didn't talk much. I suppose in some ways that was true; yet, I simply tended to only talk if I had something intelligent to say. There is nothing more annoying then listening to people talk just so they can

The Puppet Master – Page 4

hear themselves speak. If you have nothing intelligent to say, don't speak.

MARKUS: I *(Pause)* ... never mind.

ETHAN: High school was what you made it. You could be the centre of attention and in the mix of everything or you could watch the show from the sidelines. I choose the happy medium. I played on the volleyball team, was part of the SRC and, although some would say nerdy, I was on the debate team. I went to pep rallies and actually had fun; I cheered our teams on at every game and was proud to wear our school colours. That said, as much as I tried to not fall into the cliques of high school, I did.

TAMARA: I spent most of high school watching it pass me by. I didn't hate school; it was just there. I did my time, did my work and that was it. I didn't go to school activities, didn't hang out in the cafeteria and didn't go to the legendary high school parties. But in my grade 12 year, I wanted to be a part of something, to break out of my shell; Ethan did that for me.

ETHAN: Tamara was an amazing girl. I knew I had to get to know her. I knew beneath that shy exterior was a beautiful, sweet girl who was way deeper then the average girl. I liked her smile, her cute laugh and the way she chewed her hair when she was nervous. Did I love her? I don't know, what exactly is love? Isn't that the ultimate question? Either way, I knew I wanted to spend all my free time doing nothing with her.

TAMARA: Ethan was an amazing guy. On the one hand, he was witty and sarcastic; on the other hand, he was sensitive and compassionate. He volunteered at the local old folk's home, he actually enjoyed hanging out with his parents and had a blog where he ranted about the injustices of the world and what should be done to change them. Although I felt nervous around most boys, I was incredibly comfortable with Ethan. His easygoing nature allowed me to open up and be myself. With his help I became more confident, started to wear make-up, dressed a little prettier and learned to be proud of who I am. I fell in love.

ROBYN: Ever start a rumour and watch it grow? It really is a magnificent piece of work. One simple lie and the web is wove. There are very exact tips to the art of gossip. First, the more outrageous the lie, the more believable it is; second, the more innocent the target the more eagerly others believe. People love to see white turn black. Third, never, ever, let the truth come out ... the perfect lie eventually comes true.

TAMARA: *(Upset)* It can't be true, it just can't. He would never say such things.

The Puppet Master – Page 5

ETHAN: One minute our relationship was going smooth; we laughed together, cried together and already had plans to go to the same university. Me to be a lawyer and her a teacher.
TAMARA: We had talked about it for a while, a lot more lately.
ETHAN: We had dated for months; I respected her and was fine with taking it slow.
ROBYN: Did you hear that Ethan was bragging about Tamara ... and there was nothing *slow* about his comments.
TAMARA: I couldn't believe he would say that. He was always telling me he wasn't in a hurry; that he loved spending time with me ... that he loved me.
MARKUS: Dude ... nice score ... I wouldn't mind a piece of that.
ETHAN: *(Defensive)* I never said that. I was being razzed by the guys for not taking it to the next level. You know, the usual guy stuff.
'Dude what about the three date rule' or 'I bet Karen would be more than your girlfriend'.
KAREN: Guys talk the talk and then talk the talk some more. Guys are so predictable. Ninety percent of what guys say to their buddies is bogus, the other ten percent is a vague resemblance of the truth.
ROBYN: It was like a prairie fire, spreading and spreading ...
HELENA: Mirror, mirror on the wall,
Who is the baddest of them all?
MARKUS: Beer, beer in my hand,
I am your biggest fan.
ROBYN: And spreading and spreading ...
TAMARA: I was furious, how could he do this to me? Treat me as an object.
ETHAN: She would not believe me; I did not know what to do. The girls began to be malicious to her and the guys treated me as if I was some super stud. It would have been funny if it wasn't so sadly pathetic.
ROBYN: A beautiful lie can ruin, it can bring down the mighty, and it can crush the weak. Really, the perfect falsehood is a piece of art, a masterpiece. Like a well crafted Shakespearean tragedy; a Picasso; a Rembrandt.
TAMARA: Soon I had a reputation and once you are given a label it is impossible to break free. In high school, you are who you are perceived to be.
ETHAN: Tamara broke up with me and at the end of the semester transferred to another school.
KAREN: Hmmm ... Ethan is single.
HELENA: Mirror, mirror on the wall,
Another victim takes a fall ...

The Puppet Master – Page 6

ROBYN: So time went on and a new rumour spread about someone else and this one faded quickly from memory. Just like a tabloid, interesting for a while, but nothing to hold the interest for longer than the next juicy bit of gossip. Two people changed forever, and me ... amused.

SCENE TWO:

SARAH: I thought I had a relatively normal life. I wasn't really popular, nor was I unpopular. I just did my time at school, got my B marks and hung out with my few friends. I liked going to the movies, reading a good book and chatting online. I liked meeting new people online who had similar interests as me. It was the opposite of high school. Instead of being judged by my looks, clothes and zip code, I was judged by my thoughts and personality. I didn't have to pretend to be something I wasn't - like I did every day at school.

JEREMY: Life is all about rock and roll. Not the sex and drugs of the 80s, but the power of a song. A rollicking guitar riff, a five-minute drum solo, a sweet jamming session, now that is rock and roll. Real musicians, not the Justins and Britneys of the world, but the Jimmy Pages and Eric Claptons; they're hardcore. They play the music from their soul; they use blood, sweat and tears to produce a song that resonates to everyone; because true rock and roll, the kind that you can bang your head to and just let go, lasts forever. What bands last? Not the pop crap like the Backstreet Boys or Spice Girls, but straight ahead, layered guitars, pounding drums, explosive vocals, head-banging rock and roll. AC/DC, Metallica, Van Halen, The Who, The Doors, The Police, the list goes on.

MARKUS: Dude, what about Kiss? How can you not mention Kiss? They rock and roll all night. *(Laughs at his own joke)*

SARAH: Then I met Jeremy. Instantly everything changed. We immediately clicked and although we came from very different backgrounds, we were inseparable. He was funny, outgoing, secretly intelligent and the lead singer of Social Disorder, a local rock and roll band. They say opposites attract, with Jeremy and I that was definitely the case. He introduced me to many new things like rock and roll concerts, XBOX, poker ... French kissing.

MARKUS: Or Motley Crue. Motley Crue is a rock and roll must. *(Pauses and smiles)* Sarah is like super cute. I'd like to um, like, you know ... kick start her heart and be her Dr. Feelgood.

JEREMY: Sarah was my opposite - shy, conservative and in the church choir. I was outgoing, pro-active and anti-church. She helped me understand religion and although I was still very skeptical and had

The Puppet Master – Page 7

more questions than answers, I did begin to believe. Yet, none of that mattered when we were together.

KAREN: I had to laugh when I saw Sarah and Jeremy holding hands. The church snob and the slimy greaser a couple, what a hoot. I mean what next, was the quarterback going to date some lowly nerd?

ROBYN: Sometimes when I am really bored, I watch 80s movies and just laugh. The plots are always so cheesy. Like 16 Candles - a girl whose family forgets her 16th birthday, *(Sarcastic)* how tragic, like ... how does she go on?; or how about The Breakfast Club - as if one day in detention would have all the different cliques of a high school bond. Cliques stay with their own - that is just the way things are. Jocks date cheerleaders, band geeks hang out with other band geeks, nerds hang out with their computers and the slugs of society hang out in the smoking section with other slugs. So when I learned about Jeremy, the skid, and Sarah, the church girl, dating, I knew I had to do something extreme.

SARAH: High school was funny. Jeremy was stereotyped as a stoner because he had long hair, wore heavy metal concert shirts and hung out in smoker's corner. Yet, Jeremy did not smoke, drink or do drugs. He simply loved rock 'n' roll. He wrote songs about politics and social issues. Although he barely passed his classes, he was actually really smart.

JEREMY: I despised school. The classes were usually redundant and boring, except history. History was amazing. Why doesn't man realize that history repeats itself? Ghangis Khan, Napoleon, Stalin, and Hitler, all killed millions for their own personal agendas. Now we have Darfur. One thing is certain; although everything changes, nothing really changes.

SARAH: As soon as people learned we were dating, I got skeptical or quizzical looks. 'What are you doing with him?' I was asked. 'Really? You and Jeremy,' I was quizzed. Even one of my teachers questioned me about Jeremy. At first I was annoyed, but then I got angry. I was sick of being judged, I was sick of Jeremy being judged. Why does anybody care who I date?

JEREMY: As much as I disliked the classes, what I really hated were the people. The posers, the followers, the jocks, they all think the school is theirs. What a howl. In ten years, who will remember who the captain of the basketball team was? Who was named prom king and queen? What the heck was said in the valedictorian's speech? The answer ... nobody.

KAREN: Sarah was my lab partner. I wouldn't say we were good friends, but I liked her. She helped me get by in Chemistry, a course I still know nothing about. So being a friend, I suggested that dating

The Puppet Master – Page 8

Jeremy may hurt her reputation. All girls have to worry about their reputation, but she would just not listen.
MARKUS: For-a-good-time-call-Karen giving goody-goody-Sarah reputation advice ... now that is ironic. Is that the right word? Ironic. Wow, I learned something in English the third time. Cool.
SARAH: My reputation? No one at school noticed me before, why should I care about my reputation?
ROBYN: The rumor about Sarah was not actually about being malicious. It was about keeping the hierarchy of high school social status the way it should be. Sarah was technically a prep, be it a not very cool one, but still she was substantially above the worm that was Jeremy. Technically, I was doing Sarah a favor.
JEREMY: I am not sure if I was in love with Sarah, I am a guy so love is somewhat abstract to me, but I sure liked her a lot. We hadn't really done anything much. Held hands, made out, the usual. Going further had only been a fantasy in my head, often late at night if you get my drift, and the topic had not yet been broached. Next thing I know ...
KAREN: Sarah is pregnant. Debbie told Allie who told Cara who told Betty who told Danielle who told Cayley who told me that she saw Sarah leaving Dr. Wilson's office yesterday. Dr. Wilson only deals with people who have a bun in the oven so obviously ...
MARKUS: Dudes ... Jeremy is going to be a daddy. So, so, so, not cool.
SARAH: When I first heard the rumor I was pregnant, I actually laughed so hard I had tears in my eyes. Mom gave me the birds and the bees' speech, I did pretty well in biology and Jeremy and I had not had sex yet, so I was pretty darn sure I was not pregnant. Yet, the rumor would not go away.
JEREMY: When I first heard the rumor, I just chalked it up to the usual high school crap. Yet, it kept haunting me. She spent a lot of time with Martin, her best friend, and soon I began to wonder if there was something going on.
HELENA: Ring around the high schools
Pocket full of teen fools
Husha husha
They all fall down.
ROBYN: I couldn't believe my eyes. Jeremy just ripped Sarah apart in the lunchroom in front of half the school. He accused her of cheating with that geek Martin, now that is funny, and Sarah ran out of the room crying. This had gone even better than I had imagined. I thought this one might not go anywhere, but jealousy, oh, the insecurity of man, wins again.

The Puppet Master – Page 9

SCENE THREE:

MIRANDA: OK, so what, exactly, is wrong with being smart? Why is it that getting good grades is frowned on and you are automatically isolated from the so-called cool group, whatever that is? Like really, when was it decided who would be the cool kids and who would be the outcasts? Was it based on social class? Looks? Athletics? Well, I come from a poor family, I get extremely high marks and I don't know a touchdown from a home run. Yet, I am a very interesting person. The funny thing is they really have no idea who I am, what I like, my joys, my fears, my hopes and my dreams. In reality, I am a fun person to be around, if only they would look past the exterior.

MARKUS: Yeah that is likely. Could you imagine it? The guys just hanging out and checking out the chicks. 'Hey man, look at the personality on that babe.' *(Different voice)* 'Wow, I have not seen personality like that forever.' *(Normal voice)* 'Yeah man, if you play your cards right - you and her can converse all night long.' *(Different voice)* 'Sweet man. Yeah I'd love to just lay awake all night and listen to her tell me about her fears, her hopes and her dreams while we watch The Notebook.' *(Normal voice)* 'The Notebook, a classic film, man. I cry every time I see it.' *(Different voice)* 'Me too man, sometimes I just need to be held.' *(Normal voice)* 'Don't we all. Come here man, I'll give you a hug.' *(Pause)* As if!

CHANCE: People assume that because you are the quarterback, your parents are rich and you are rather attractive, that life is just peachy. Yeah right. My dad is a doctor and expects I should go to Harvard for my doctorial, just because he did, and, of course, play football. My mom drinks a lot; my parents' marriage is a charade and slowly the pretending she is happy facade is wearing her down. Lastly, I do not even want to be a doctor, I want to be an actor. Not that anyone has ever asked.

KAREN: Chance is so fine, delicious eye candy.

MARKUS: Dude ... Karen has like ... so been around the block ... like I even tapped that.

ROBYN: Funny how sometimes gossip can backfire. There was this girl Miranda, a real nerd. She usually wore her hair in pigtails, always had her head in a book and always wore clothes from Walmart. Walmart for Pete's sake. So I thought for fun I would get Dave, a friend of mine, to write her a love letter or two that I'd dictate and leave unsigned. Well for a week or two I could barely contain myself when I saw her read each new letter.

HELENA: Roses are red, violets are blue,
Sinister dealings, deja vu.

The Puppet Master – Page 10

MIRANDA: At first I thought the letters were a joke. They were signed secret admirer, and I just kept waiting for the punch line. Like really, who could like me?
MARKUS: Your parents?
MIRANDA: But soon I began to be swept away with the eloquence of the words. And although deep down I figured I was being set up for a fall, my hopes of love, of fitting in, took control.
CHANCE: Miranda was a sweet girl. She made me laugh and she was a great partner to have. I enjoyed working on the chemistry project with her; we really clicked working together.
ROBYN: Well guess what, a brilliant idea came to mind. When I learned that shy Miranda and the football star Chance, the pretty boy of the school, were partners, I figured this was too good to be true. So guess what we did? Yeah we did. We wrote another letter and signed it Chance. Then we waited for the hysterics to begin.
KAREN: Figures, the nerd always gets put with the hot guy. She probably thinks second base is only in baseball.
MIRANDA: The fourth letter was the most romantic yet. It said my eyes lit up the room and that I was the only star of his universe. It was signed Chance.
CHANCE: Well soon I began to have feelings for Miranda. She was more than just a superficial waif like the usual girls I dated. She had substance, she had intelligence, she had wit, she had a quick sense of humour and behind that insecurity and conservativeness lay a beautiful girl ... waiting to bloom.
HELENA: Roses are red, violets are blue,
True love hit and cupid had no clue.
MARKUS: Roses are red, pot is green,
I'm every girl's living dream.
MIRANDA: My knees quivered as I wondered what I should say, what I should do. Sure I had been crazy about him since I was in grade six, but never even considered it more than a school girl's fantasy.
CHANCE: So, at the end of class one day, I decided to ask her out.
MIRANDA: When he asked me out it was like slow motion. I still remember the look in his eyes, the sincerity, the twinkle, the blue. I remember how every insecurity I had vanished and how I struggled to say yes, even though in my head I was screaming it so loud it echoed.
KAREN: As if, what is she some sort of charity case? Why would Chance date a revolting freakoid when someone like me, a cheerleader, is available?
MARKUS: Like why do I never get the chicks? Look at me, who does not want a piece of this?

The Puppet Master – Page 11

CHANCE: She was everything I wanted ... and needed. She taught me to be who I am and to stand up for myself. I think I taught her the same thing.
ROBYN: You got to be kidding me. Oh well, on to my next victim.
HELENA: Roses are red, violets are blue,
True love always follows through.

SCENE FOUR:

ADAM: The letting go of anger has three stages. The first stage is allowing the anger to build. This pent-up fury slowly increases inside of you until you feel a rage that you can no longer control. Sanity slowly dissolves till you are left without reasoning or logic. Instead, the anger consumes you until it must be released. The second stage is the releasing of the anger. The anger explodes out of you like a volcano after years of being dormant. How the anger is released varies, but always there is a victim who receives the full extent of the wrath. It might be a girlfriend, a parent, a wall, your own body, but it must be released on something for it to occur. The third stage is regret. Almost immediately after the anger is released, there is a sudden wave of regret as the individual realizes that the outlet of their anger was wrongly directed. Of course, the cycle continues over and over and over again - each time the anger becoming more explosive as the issue never gets solved.
TISH: Have you ever been so angry that you just snap? So angry that all you want to do is cry, but no tears ever come? That is how I feel all the time. No matter how hard I try to let go of the past, to forget, the angrier I get. I have cried till I no longer have tears, I have punched and punched till my hands bled and I have screamed and yelled every profanity I know; yet, I never feel better, every day I hate myself and my life more and more.
ADAM: Tish and I met at an anger management seminar at school. Both of us forced there to "deal" with our issues. We had to go or be expelled from school. I thought about not going, but I knew my dad would give me another beating if I was expelled, so I reluctantly went.
TISH: The seminar was intense. There were six of us at this mandatory counselling session and by the end of the day I felt better and worse. In some ways hearing people who are worse off than me, made me feel better; yet, on the other hand, my problems did not magically go away after one day of therapy.
MARKUS: I have something that would make all your problems magically go away. *(Pause)* A special brownie.

The Puppet Master – Page 12

ADAM: I couldn't believe the things I heard. A girl who found her dad after he committed suicide and still blamed herself; a guy who was so heavy into drugs he shook the whole day slowly getting more agitated minute by minute.

TISH: Then there was Adam. He barely spoke all day, refusing to acknowledge the pain he obviously was feeling. Yet, as the day went on, I began to sense he wanted to be heard, wanted to tell his story.

ADAM: Although I didn't say anything revealing the whole day, it was somewhat therapeutic. I realized I was not the only one with problems, nor the only one who did not know how to handle their problems; but no matter how hard I tried to open up, no words came out. Though, after hearing Tish tell her story, I felt a connection, the slightest flicker of a spark, a spark I had not felt for a long time.

TISH: My dad left when I was seven. He left the same day I got into trouble for getting into a fight at school. When I came home he was gone. No matter how much my mom told me it was not my fault, I always blamed myself. Maybe if I were more this, or more that, then maybe daddy wouldn't have left. Obviously, I realized over time that his leaving had nothing to do with me, but that kind of hurt never leaves. My mother never got over the betrayal either. She slowly became a shadow of her former self. I became the adult of the family, looking after my two younger sisters. I got them awake in the morning, fed them breakfast, brushed their teeth and got them off to school, while my mother slept through her drunken slumber. Over time, my hate continued to grow and grow, spinning in circles, searching for a way to break free.

ADAM: So I asked her to go for coffee with me, I felt we had similar problems. The characters were different, but the plot was the same. My mom left my dad, my younger brother and me when I was 10. I blamed everyone. My mom for not standing up to my dad all those long years, my younger brother for being such a cry baby, my dad for being such a drunk, violent bastard and me … for not protecting the ones I loved.

TISH: I honestly did not want to say yes, but I saw a need in his eyes, a silent desperation. But after a few coffee dates he began to slowly, ever so slowly, open up. I saw a young man who hated his dad and hated himself.

ADAM: I had never told anyone that my dad used me as his own personal punching bag, his own anger therapy. He always apologized next day, but next time he was drunk the fist eventually connected with my body. I would never allow father dearest to hit Tyler; I had to protect him. Yet, my anger boiled inside of me, begging to be unleashed.

The Puppet Master – Page 13

TISH: Before I knew it, I was in love with him. We had a bond, a secret understanding; we knew what each other were feeling without words. He understood my pain, my anger towards my mother. He kept me calm when I was ready to break. He began to heal a wound I never felt could be healed. He loved me, when I never thought I would be loved. Yet, there were other times when he felt distant, distracted, lost.

MARKUS: I feel that way all the time baby, all the time.

ADAM: Stats say something like nine out of ten people who are abused as children, end up being abusive to their children. Those stats scared the crap out of me. I did not want to be like my father. I had to find a way to squelch the serpent trying to break free from inside of me.

ROBYN: Some people heal a broken heart with ice cream; others by finding a new hottie; others deal with it in crying fits; while others deal with it with insecure blame games - 'oh if only I would have put out or been a little skinnier'. Me, I get revenge. When Adam dumped me I was furious. He never gave me a reason, just said it wasn't working and he needed to spend more time at home. What kind of excuse is that? Anyways, it took some time, over a year, but when I learned that Adam and that loopy Tish were getting friendly, well I saw my chance for payback.

KAREN: I had the hots for Adam forever. He was so handsome, so mysterious.

MARKUS: Karen had the hots for any guy who breathed.

ROBYN: To make matters better, I heard that easy stuck up cheerleader Karen wanted to make a play for my Adam. So at the usual Friday night party, the perfect play was executed. Adam was at the party with his buddies and I learned that Tish was not going to be there till she got off of work at 11. So I slipped the rumor and watched it cultivate.

MARKUS: Dude, did you hear that dirty cheerleader Karen and that pretty boy, what's his name, Mike, no, um, Wally, no, um, Adam, yeah ... Adam were like ... making out upstairs.

ROBYN: The rumor spread quickly and just as it got to Karen, Tish came in right on cue. The rumor, or as far as she knew, the truth, was whispered to her in seconds of her arrival.

HELENA: Easy come, easy go,
  Tish's fuse is about to blow.

MARKUS: Easy come, easy go,
  Sweet, time for a show.

TISH: When I was told about Karen seducing Adam I flipped. All those years of pent-up frustration came to a head and without thinking I found Karen and punched her in the face. Again and again, I hit her;

The Puppet Master – Page 14

I was pulled off her by a group of guys and restrained. The look of shock on Karen's face instantly told me it was not true. But how do you say sorry? How do you explain that I was not hitting her, but my mother? That she was just the victim of years and years of my lost youth.

MARKUS: Dude ... that was like ... the coolest thing ever.

ROBYN: The night was not done yet, not by a long shot. After the catfight was stopped by the jocks, Adam snapped on everyone.

HELENA: Easy come, easy go,
Time to hit, an all-time low.

ADAM: After seeing Tish break, I did too. I didn't want to, but it was like my body was being led without my permission. I threw the vase against the wall, I shattered a mirror with a beer bottle and I started cursing and yelling at everyone at the party. 'Why do we all hate each other? Why can't we just respect each other's differences and get along? Why do we always expect the worst out of each other?' As I said it, I already knew the answer. Because no matter how much our lives suck, how much pain we are in, it makes us feel better to see others suffer too. It means there are people worse off than us. And although that is a hollow comfort, it still is comfort.

SCENE FIVE: EPILOGUE

HELENA: Time moves on
Five years have passed
The world keeps turning
Robyn gets the last laugh.

TAMARA: I learned a couple years later that the rumour was indeed not true. By then it was too late, my first love was stolen from me. I have tried to call him and apologize for everything, but I can not get up the nerve.

ETHAN: I tried for a long time to convince her it was a lie. That I loved her and would never have done such an awful thing. Yet, our lives were changed forever. I still think about her on occasion. I always wonder ... what if?

JEREMY: In the end, I too succumbed to the idiocies of high school. I jumped to irrational conclusions and by the time I realized the obvious, it was too late. You can't take back words, they linger long after they are said ... like a fog off the ocean coast.

SARAH: Jeremy eventually came around and realized he was wrong and apologized to me. I accepted his apology, but I could no longer see him in the same light. The anger and hate he threw at me that

The Puppet Master – Page 15

day hit me like a thousand daggers and although I forgave him, I could not forget.

TISH: I knew after that night I had to leave home. I had to break free from the hold my mother's guilt had over me. I did the hardest thing I have ever had to do, I phoned social services. My siblings were eventually placed in a nice home together, while I ended up bouncing around from shelter to shelter. I never did graduate high school, but after years of soul-searching I have discovered who I am: a young woman simply trying to find her place in the world.

ADAM: That night changed me forever. My anger finally overwhelmed me and almost turned me into something I never wanted to be, my father. The fury did not make me feel better, only made me feel like a monster, a freak. I knew I needed help and although I still have a long way to go, I have come to accept my weaknesses and learned how to overcome them. I have come to the obvious revelation that my father will never change, but I can ...

KAREN: In retrospect, high school brought out the worst in me. I enjoyed being the centre of attention and hearing the latest juicy piece of gossip, but I spent way too much time worrying what others thought of me and not enough time worrying what was best for me. The next big rumour at school was that I was pregnant; unfortunately this rumour was true. I got my grade 12, barely, and instead of going to college like all my friends, I still live at home raising my son.

MIRANDA: A couple months later, I learned that Chance had not written those letters. I often wondered who did, yet it really did not matter. Chance and I would spend every free second we could together. I supported Chance and told him to do what he wanted to do.

CHANCE: *(Yelling)* Dad, I am not going to be your puppet. I am not like you. *(Relaxed now)* My dad was furious at first. An actor? It took some time for him to come around, but in the end it made our relationship stronger. I can thank Miranda for that. She is my everything. I asked her to marry me last week. It seemed like the right time. We have dated for five years and I just got my first big break; a lead role in a Broadway version of Hamlet. *(In a British accent)* I am Horatio.

MARKUS: Dude ... high school was like the best six years of my life. One more year and I would have, like so, graduated.

ROBYN: The art of gossip is an exact science. The styles of gossip spreading can also vary. Sometimes a situation that is already tepid can be pushed to a confrontation with a little well worded gossip. Other times a well spread tidbit of false information can forever taint a person's reputation. Of course, the best revenge is a dish best served with malicious gossip. It is sooooo beautiful; all the pleasure

The Puppet Master – Page 16

      of revenge, all the anger unleashed and it never gets back to the one who started it. Perfection. I am the puppet master.
CHANCE: Oh yeah, she said yes.
HELENA: It was the best of times
    It was the worst of times
    It was the time of perseverance
    Where everything was based on appearance
    Lives were shattered-tainted forever
    All for the sinister pleasure
    Of the puppet master who set the fire
    And watched as the flames went higher
    She smiled, laughed and gave an evil grin
    As she bathed in the glory of her sin.

ROBYN: *(Laughs evilly)*

(CURTAIN FALLS)

                END OF PLAY

The Puppet Master – Page 17

STAGE SET-UP SUGGESTIONS:

VERSION 1

    Markus   Robyn   Helena   Karen

                            (on risers)

Tamara Sarah Miranda Tish Adam Chance Jeremy Ethan

VERSION 2

    Markus   Robyn   Helena   Karen

                            (on risers)

Tamara Ethan Miranda Chance Tish Adam Sarah Jeremy

VERSION 3

                            Robyn

                  Markus   Karen

              Adam   Tish

          Chance   Miranda

      Jeremy   Sarah

Ethan   Tamara

                                  Helena

The Puppet Master – Page 18

COSTUMES

All characters are seniors in high school. Below are suggestions for outfitting the cast, but obviously the director and cast may very well have a different vision of the characters.

MARKUS: Would dress in ripped jeans, a t-shirt and a leather jacket.

HELENA: Would probably wear all black, skirt, clearly an artist.

KAREN: Would dress in a cheerleading outfit or in an outfit that would be somewhat provocative.

ROBYN: Would probably dress in a black skirt, black pantyhose, heels and a tight fitting blouse ... she needs to have a distinct, I am better then everyone else, look from the rest of the cast.

TAMARA: Hair may be in a ponytail; would dress rather conservatively, for example a sweater and jeans.

ETHAN: Would dress casual-jeans and a t-shirt.

SARAH: Would dress casual-a blouse and jeans.

JEREMY: Would dress in jeans, a heavy metal 80s t-shirt, Van Halen perhaps, and a bandanna.

MIRANDA: Would probably wear a sundress or a long skirt and blouse - likely she would wear glasses.

CHANCE: Would wear a football jersey and jeans or a sports team jacket.

ADAM: Would likely dress preppy in khakis and a dress shirt.

TISH: Would dress to hide how attractive she actually is-a bulky sweatshirt, sweatpants and a ball cap; she could have more stylish clothes underneath and part way through the scene take off the ball cap, sweatshirt and sweatpants to reveal a more confident side (like a skirt and a blouse or jeans and a flattering shirt.)

The Puppet Master – Page 19

NOTES

NOTES